Estate Planning Essentials: A Beginners Guide

David Scott Russ, Esq.

Copyright © 2023 David Scott Russ

All rights reserved.

ISBN: 9798862281095

DEDICATION

For Maurice, continue to grow.

CONTENTS

	Acknowledgments	i
1	Understanding Estate Planning	1
2	Setting Your Estate Planning Goals	Pg 10
3	Creating a Will	Pg 14
4	Trusts: A Versatile Planning Tool	Pg 18
5	Estate and Gift Tax	Pg 22
6	Beneficiary Designations	Pg 25
7	Advanced Healthcare Directives and Powers of Attorney	Pg 28
8	Review and Update Your Estate Plan	Pg 31
9	Conclusion	Pg 34
	Planning Outline	Pg 36

ACKNOWLEDGMENTS

This book is a collection of the knowledge of other attorneys in addition to years of the author's own practice and experience, supplemented with case law and statutes of certain states. The language used in this book is meant to be as detailed as possible while staying as general as possible to all states and their laws. The author is licensed to practice in North Carolina, so the applicability of detailed legal concepts or statutory authority may not extend to your state. Nothing in this book is intended as legal advice as each individual reader may have different circumstances that require specifically tailored legal representation. Purchase of this book does not create any attorney-client relationship, nor does it obligate the author or publisher to represent you in the creation, administration or defense of your estate plan. You are encouraged to contact an attorney in your state when you feel it is time to create a comprehensive estate plan for yourself or your family.

CHAPTER 1:
UNDERSTANDING ESTATE PLANNING

Estate planning is not just a financial matter; it's a holistic approach to securing your future and ensuring your legacy lives on. In this chapter, we'll delve into the essential components of estate planning, shedding light on what it encompasses and why it matters. By the end of this chapter, you'll have a solid grasp of the fundamental concepts that underpin estate planning, setting the stage for the more detailed discussions that follow.

Estate: Defining the Scope of Your Legacy

Your estate is the sum total of everything you own, from the tangible to the intangible. It comprises your physical possessions, financial assets, and even your debts and obligations. Understanding your estate's scope is the first step in estate planning. In this section, we will explore:

- Tangible Assets: Your home, real estate, vehicles, jewelry, art, and personal belongings.
- Financial Assets: Bank accounts, investments, retirement accounts, life insurance, and business interests. This can also include non-traditional assets such as NFTs and digital currency such as Bitcoin.
- Debts and Liabilities: Mortgages, loans, credit card debts, and any other financial obligations.

ESTATE PLANNING BASICS: A BEGINNERS GUIDE

Knowing the full extent of your estate and the assets of which it is comprised is crucial because it forms the basis for decisions about its distribution and protection and is the most important step in creating an estate plan. Not addressing a specific asset or class of assets can cause confusion and unintended distributions.

Tangible Assets: Defining the Scope of Your Physical Possessions

Tangible assets encompass the physical belongings and properties you own. It's essential to understand their value and how they fit into your estate plan. Here are some suggestions to address tangible assets:

1. Create a Detailed Inventory: Compile a comprehensive list of your tangible assets, including your primary residence, vacation properties, vehicles, jewelry, antiques, art, furniture, and personal belongings of significant value. Digital tools or spreadsheets can help organize this information efficiently.

2. Appraise High-Value Items: For valuable items like jewelry, art, or collectibles, consider having them appraised by professionals to determine their current market value. This appraisal will help ensure their fair distribution among your beneficiaries.

3. Determine Distribution Preferences: Decide how you want to distribute these tangible assets among your beneficiaries. You can be specific about who gets what or provide general guidelines for equitable distribution.

4. Consider Sentimental Value: Some items may not have significant monetary value but hold sentimental importance to you or your loved ones. Discuss these sentimental items with your beneficiaries to understand their preferences and factor them into your plan.

5. Plan for Special Handling: Certain assets may require unique handling, such as caring for pets, maintaining a family cabin, or ensuring the upkeep of valuable collections. Include provisions in your estate plan for these assets to ensure they are properly managed.

Financial Assets: Understanding Your Monetary Holdings

Financial assets include various forms of investments, accounts, and interests that make up a significant portion of your estate. Properly accounting for these assets is crucial for estate planning. Here are some suggestions:

1. Gather Financial Statements: Collect statements for all your financial accounts, including bank accounts, investment portfolios, retirement accounts (e.g., 401(k) or IRAs), and life insurance policies.

2. Assess Asset Allocation: Review your investment portfolio and consider how it aligns with your overall estate plan and risk tolerance. You may need to rebalance or adjust your investments to better meet your goals.

3. Update Beneficiary Designations: Ensure that beneficiary designations on accounts like retirement plans and life insurance policies accurately reflect your current wishes. Changes in your family or personal circumstances may necessitate updates.

4. Plan for Business Interests: If you own a business or have a stake in one, outline your intentions for its future, whether it's passing it on to family members, selling it, or designating a successor.

5. Consider Liquidity Needs: Assess your estate's liquidity, as some assets may not be easily convertible to cash. You may need to plan for potential cash flow requirements, such as paying off debts, taxes, or estate administration expenses.

Debts and Liabilities: Addressing Financial Obligations

Debts and liabilities are often overlooked aspects of estate planning but can significantly affect the distribution of your assets. Here's how to address these financial obligations:

1. Compile a List of Debts: Make a comprehensive list of all your outstanding debts, including mortgages, personal loans, credit card balances, and any other financial obligations. Specify the creditors and the outstanding balances.

2. Review Co-Signed or Joint Debts: If you share debts with someone else (e.g., a spouse or business partner), discuss how these joint obligations will be handled in your estate plan.

3. Life Insurance and Debt Coverage: Consider whether your life insurance policies provide sufficient coverage to pay off your debts upon your passing. Ensuring that your beneficiaries won't be burdened by your debts is an important aspect of estate planning.

4. Set Aside Funds for Debt Repayment: If your estate does not have sufficient liquidity to cover your debts, consider allocating specific assets or funds from your estate to cover these obligations. This can help prevent the forced sale of assets to settle debts.

5. Review Estate's Solvency: Periodically assess your estate's solvency, ensuring that your assets outweigh your debts. Adjust your estate plan as needed to maintain a healthy financial balance.

By addressing tangible assets, financial assets, and debts and liabilities in your estate plan, you'll have a comprehensive understanding of your estate's scope. This clarity enables you to make informed decisions about how to distribute your assets, minimize tax liabilities, and protect the financial well-being of your loved ones. Additionally, regularly reviewing and updating this information as your circumstances change is essential to maintaining an effective estate plan.

Beneficiaries: Determining Your Legacy's Recipients

One of the core objectives of estate planning is to ensure your assets pass on to the individuals or entities you intend. These intended recipients are known as beneficiaries. In developing a comprehensive estate plan, most people

consider the following as potential beneficiaries:
- Family Members: Spouses, children, grandchildren, and other relatives who depend on your support.
- Friends: Close friends who hold a special place in your life.
- Charities and Organizations: Non-profit organizations and causes you wish to support.
- Specific Individuals: If you have step-children, godchildren, godparents, or close friends without blood ties, you can include them as beneficiaries too.

Choosing your beneficiaries carefully and clearly documenting your intentions is a critical aspect of estate planning. Your choices can greatly impact the lives of those you leave behind.

Executor: The Guardian of Your Wishes

When you've determined how you want your estate distributed, you'll need someone you trust to carry out these wishes. This person is known as the executor or personal representative. In selecting a proper executor, it is necessary to consider and understand the following:
- Responsibilities of an Executor: The role involves managing the administrative tasks of your estate, including filing legal documents, distributing assets, and paying debts and taxes.
- Qualities of a Good Executor: Trustworthiness, organization, and financial acumen are some essential qualities to consider when selecting an executor.
- Formally Naming an Executor: The process of appointing an executor involves careful consideration and clarity in the documentation, as this individual will play a pivotal role in realizing your estate plan.

In some situations, it may be advisable to name more than one executor so that the obligations and responsibilities are shared by those named to act on behalf of the estate. This can reduce workload on any one individual and potentially expedite the probate administration of your estate. On the other hand, naming two or more people to act as co-executors can create unnecessary delay and friction as it is often the requirement of the court that all co-executors sign documents that are necessary for the administration of the estate. This paper-shuffling can slow the process.

Your choice of an executor is crucial, as they will ensure your wishes are faithfully executed, making it essential to select someone who is not only competent but also aligned with your values and preferences.

Probate: The Legal Process of Estate Administration

Probate is a legal process that involves validating a will and overseeing the distribution of assets according to its terms. Understanding probate is essential because it can have a significant impact on the efficiency and cost-effectiveness of your estate plan. In this section, we'll briefly explore:

- The Probate Process: A step-by-step overview of what happens during probate, including the validation of the will, the inventory of assets, and the distribution of assets.
- Costs and Delays: Probate can be expensive and time-consuming, potentially reducing the assets available for your beneficiaries.
- Avoiding Probate: Strategies to minimize or bypass probate, such as creating living trusts and structuring your assets strategically.

By grasping the complexities and potential drawbacks of probate, you'll be better equipped to make informed decisions about your estate plan and explore options that can streamline the process.

Understanding the Probate Process in Estate Planning

Probate is a legal process that serves to validate a deceased person's will and facilitate the orderly distribution of their assets to beneficiaries. While probate ensures that assets are transferred according to the deceased's wishes, it can also be associated with costs, delays, and public scrutiny. It's crucial for estate planning clients to comprehend this process fully to make informed decisions about their estate plans. Probate typically involves several key steps:

1. Validation of the Will: The probate court will examine the will to

ESTATE PLANNING BASICS: A BEGINNERS GUIDE

ensure it is legally valid. This includes confirming that it meets the state's requirements regarding witnesses and the testator's mental capacity.

2. Appointment of an Executor: If an executor is named in the will, the court will appoint them to oversee the probate process. If no executor is named, the court will appoint an administrator.

3. Inventory of Assets: The executor or administrator is responsible for creating an inventory of the deceased's assets, which includes valuing and documenting each asset. This can be a time-consuming task.

4. Notification of Creditors: Creditors have the opportunity to make claims against the estate. The executor must notify known creditors and may need to publish notices in local newspapers to inform potential creditors.

5. Payment of Debts and Taxes: Debts, taxes, and administrative expenses are paid from the estate's assets before distribution to beneficiaries.

6. Distribution of Assets: After debts and expenses are settled, the remaining assets are distributed to beneficiaries according to the terms of the will.

Suggestion: To streamline this process, maintain well-organized records of assets, debts, and estate-related documents. Consider naming an executor you trust or consult with an attorney experienced in estate planning to guide you through this complex process.

Costs and Delays

Probate can be costly and time-consuming, which may ultimately red·   ·he assets available for your beneficiaries. The costs associated with p⸢ include court fees, attorney fees, executor fees, and appraisal ⸌ can arise due to court schedules, creditor claims, and the ⸌ complete the required legal procedures.

Suggestion: To mitigate these costs and delays, consider the following:

1. Create a Living Trust: Transfer assets into a revocable living trust during your lifetime to bypass probate entirely. This allows for a smoother and more private asset distribution.

2. Plan Your Estate Carefully: Consult with an experienced estate planning attorney to structure your estate plan in a way that minimizes probate costs. This may include using beneficiary designations, joint ownership, and payable-on-death accounts.

3. Update Your Plan Regularly: Keep your estate plan up to date to ensure it accurately reflects your wishes and accounts for changes in laws or circumstances that might affect probate.

Avoiding Probate: Strategies to Minimize or Bypass Probate

There are various strategies to minimize or bypass the probate process altogether:

1. Living Trusts: As mentioned, a revocable living trust allows you to transfer assets to the trust during your lifetime, with instructions on how they should be distributed upon your passing. Assets held in the trust do not go through probate.

2. Joint Ownership: Holding assets jointly with rights of survivorship can help assets pass directly to the surviving owner without going through probate.

3. Beneficiary Designations: For assets like retirement accounts and life insurance policies, naming beneficiaries can ensure they receive the assets directly, avoiding probate.

4. Transfer-on-Death (TOD) and Payable-on-Death (POD) Accounts: Some financial accounts allow you to designate beneficiaries who automatically inherit the assets upon your death.

5. Small Estate Procedures: In some jurisdictions, estates of a certain size may qualify for simplified, expedited probate procedures or even exemption from probate.

Suggestion: Work with an estate planning attorney to determine the most appropriate strategies for your specific situation. The optimal approach may involve a combination of these methods to minimize the impact of probate on your estate.

Understanding the probate process is a crucial element of estate planning. By comprehending the steps involved, recognizing the potential costs and delays, and exploring strategies to avoid or minimize probate, you can make informed decisions that align with your goals for asset distribution and legacy planning. Consulting with an experienced estate planning attorney can provide valuable guidance in navigating this complex aspect of estate planning.

Chapter 1 – The Big Picture

Estate planning is a multifaceted endeavor that extends beyond simply deciding who gets what. It encompasses understanding the full scope of your estate, selecting beneficiaries, appointing a trustworthy executor, and considering ways to minimize the impact of probate. This chapter has laid the groundwork for your estate planning journey by introducing these key concepts. As you proceed through this book, you'll gain a deeper understanding of how to navigate the intricacies of estate planning and secure your legacy for generations to come

CHAPTER 2:
SETTING YOUR ESTATE PLANNING GOALS

Setting clear estate planning goals is the foundation of a well-structured estate plan. These goals provide direction, help prioritize your objectives, and ensure your wishes are met. In this chapter, we will touch on each common estate planning goal and offer suggestions for addressing them.

Providing for Loved Ones

Concern: Ensuring the financial security and well-being of your loved ones is often a primary estate planning goal, particularly if you have dependents such as children or disabled family members.

Suggestions:
1. Life Insurance: Consider purchasing life insurance policies to provide a financial safety net for your family in the event of your unexpected passing.
2. Will or Trust: Create a will or trust that clearly outlines how your assets will be distributed to provide for your loved ones. Name guardians for minor children if necessary.
3. Educational Planning: If you have children, plan for their education expenses through dedicated accounts or provisions in your estate

plan.

Minimizing Taxes

Concern: Estate taxes can significantly reduce the amount of assets passed on to your beneficiaries.

Suggestions:
1. Know the Tax Threshold: Be aware of the estate tax threshold, both federally and in your jurisdiction and plan your estate to stay below it if possible. The current Federal Estate Tax threshold (2023) is quite high, but is expected to sunset to a much lower level and this threshold has historically been subject to frequent legislative modification.
2. Gifts: Take advantage of the annual gift tax exclusion to reduce the size of your taxable estate by gifting assets to your beneficiaries during your lifetime.
3. Irrevocable Trusts: Explore the use of irrevocable trusts to remove assets from your taxable estate.
4. Estate Tax Planning Strategies: Consult with a tax professional or estate planning attorney to implement tax-efficient strategies tailored to your situation.

Avoiding Probate

Concern: Probate can be a time-consuming and costly process, potentially tying up assets for months or even years and adding tens of thousands of dollars to the administrative costs of even the most modest estate.

Suggestions:
1. Living Trust: Create a revocable living trust to transfer assets outside of probate. You retain control during your lifetime, and assets in the trust pass directly to beneficiaries upon your passing.
2. Beneficiary Designations: Use beneficiary designations for accounts like retirement plans and life insurance to bypass probate.
3. Joint Ownership: Hold assets jointly with rights of survivorship to enable seamless transfer to the surviving owner without probate.

ESTATE PLANNING BASICS: A BEGINNERS GUIDE

4. Small Estate Procedures: Inquire if your jurisdiction has simplified probate procedures for smaller estates.

Healthcare Planning

Concern: In the event of incapacity, it's crucial to have a plan for your healthcare preferences and who will make medical decisions on your behalf.

Suggestions:
1. Advance Healthcare Directive: Create a legally binding document that outlines your medical treatment preferences, including decisions about life-sustaining treatments.
2. Durable Power of Attorney for Healthcare: Appoint a trusted individual as your healthcare agent to make medical decisions for you if you're unable to do so.
3. Discuss Your Wishes: Communicate your healthcare preferences with your family and healthcare agent to ensure your desires are understood.

Charitable Giving

Concern: Many individuals wish to support causes and organizations they care about through planned charitable donations.

Suggestions:
1. Charitable Remainder Trust: Consider setting up a charitable remainder trust to provide income to you or a beneficiary while ultimately benefiting a charity.
2. Donor-Advised Funds: Establish a donor-advised fund to make tax-deductible contributions to charities over time.
3. Include Charities in Your Will or Trust: Clearly specify your charitable beneficiaries in your estate planning documents.

Chapter 2 – The Big Picture:
Remember, estate planning is not one-size-fits-all. Your goals and strategies should align with your unique circumstances, financial situation, and personal values. Consult with an experienced estate planning attorney or financial

advisor to ensure that your goals are properly addressed in your estate plan. Additionally, regularly review and update your estate plan to reflect any changes in your life or financial situation, ensuring that your goals remain in focus and up to date.

CHAPTER 3:
CREATING A WILL

Creating a last will and testament is a critical step in estate planning, as it allows you to express your wishes for asset distribution not addressed by other testamentary documents and for the care of loved ones after your passing. To ensure that your will effectively carries out your intentions, consider the following expanded information and suggestions:

Consult an Attorney

Concern: While it's technically possible to create a will without legal assistance, it's advisable to consult an estate planning attorney, especially for complex situations.

Suggestions:
1. Legal Expertise: Estate planning laws can be intricate, and they vary by jurisdiction. An experienced attorney can navigate these laws, ensuring your will complies with state-specific requirements.
2. Tailored Advice: An attorney can offer personalized advice based on your unique circumstances, such as estate tax considerations, blended families, or charitable giving goals.
3. Avoiding Legal Pitfalls: Legal professionals can help you avoid

common mistakes that may invalidate your will or lead to disputes among beneficiaries.

List Your Assets

Concern: To create an effective will, you need to have a comprehensive understanding of your assets.

Suggestions:
1. Detailed Inventory: Create a detailed list of your assets, including bank accounts, investment accounts, real estate, vehicles, valuable personal property (e.g., jewelry, art), and digital assets.
2. Location of Documents: Keep important documents, such as deeds, titles, and financial account statements, organized and easily accessible. Provide your executor with a clear record of where to find these documents.
3. Valuation: Consider periodically valuing your assets, especially those subject to fluctuations in value, to ensure your will accurately reflects their worth.

Appoint an Executor

Concern: Your executor plays a pivotal role in executing your will and managing your estate.

Suggestions:
1. Trustworthiness: Choose an executor you trust implicitly, as they will have access to your financial information and assets.
2. Competency: Ensure your executor is capable of handling the responsibilities involved, including asset distribution, paying debts and taxes, and managing estate administration.
3. Communication: Clearly communicate your wishes and expectations with your chosen executor. It's advisable to appoint an alternate executor in case your first choice is unable or unwilling to serve.

Name Beneficiaries

Concern: Clearly specifying your beneficiaries and their respective inheritances is essential to avoid disputes and ensure your assets are distributed as you intend.

Suggestions:
1. Clarity: Be explicit in your will about who should receive which assets and in what proportions. Vague language can lead to confusion and disputes.
2. Contingency Plans: Consider including contingent beneficiaries in case your primary beneficiaries predecease you or are unable to inherit for any reason.
3. Charitable Bequests: If you wish to leave assets to charitable organizations, specify the charities, their contact information, and the assets they should receive.

Include Guardianship Provisions

Concern: If you have minor children or adult dependents with special needs, naming a guardian is crucial to ensure their care in case both parents and caregivers are unable to do so.

Suggestions:
1. Guardian Selection: Select a guardian who shares your values and can provide a stable and loving environment for your children.
2. Discuss with Potential Guardians: Before naming someone as a guardian, discuss your intentions with them to ensure they are willing to assume this responsibility.
3. Temporary Guardian: Consider appointing a temporary guardian in case your chosen guardian cannot immediately take on the role.

Sign and Execute

Concern: The proper execution of your will is crucial to ensure it's legally valid and enforceable.

Suggestions:
1. Legal Requirements: Comply with your state's legal requirements for

a valid will. These requirements typically involve signing your will in the presence of witnesses and, in some cases, a notary public.
2. Witnesses: Choose witnesses who are not beneficiaries in your will to avoid potential conflicts of interest.
3. Keep Originals Safe: Store the original copy of your will in a secure location, such as a fireproof safe or with your attorney. Inform your executor of its location and provide them with a copy.

Chapter 3 – The Big Picture:

Creating a will is a significant step in estate planning, and the guidance of an attorney can help ensure your will accurately reflects your wishes and complies with applicable laws. Regularly review and update your will to account for changes in your assets, family situation, or estate planning goals. Properly executed, your will can provide peace of mind that your loved ones and assets will be taken care of according to your desires.

CHAPTER 4
TRUSTS: A VERSATILE PLANNING TOOL

Trusts are indeed powerful and versatile tools in estate planning, offering a range of benefits to help you achieve your financial and personal objectives. Let's explore each of these common types of trusts in more detail with key elements of each and suggestions for avoiding pitfalls common to their implementation:

Revocable Living Trusts

1. Control During Your Lifetime: With a revocable living trust, you maintain control over your assets during your lifetime as both the grantor (the person who creates the trust) and the trustee (the person who manages the trust's assets).
2. Avoiding Probate: Assets placed in this trust typically bypass probate, facilitating a faster and more private transfer of assets to beneficiaries upon your passing.
3. Flexibility: You can amend or revoke the trust as long as you are mentally competent, providing flexibility to adapt to changing circumstances.

Suggestions:

1. Funding the Trust: Ensure you properly fund the trust by re-titling assets in the trust's name. Without proper funding, the trust may not achieve its intended purpose.
2. Successor Trustee: Designate a trusted successor trustee who can take over the management of the trust assets if you become incapacitated or pass away.
3. Professional Assistance: Consult with an attorney experienced in trust planning to draft the trust document and guide you through the process.

Irrevocable Trusts

1. Asset Protection: Once assets are placed in an irrevocable trust, they are no longer considered part of your taxable estate. This can reduce your estate tax liability and protect assets from creditors.
2. Loss of Control: Unlike revocable trusts, irrevocable trusts typically cannot be modified or revoked without the consent of the beneficiaries.
3. Estate Tax Benefits: Irrevocable trusts can be structured to leverage estate tax exemptions and minimize the tax burden on your estate.

Suggestions:
1. Professional Guidance: Consult with an experienced estate planning attorney to create and manage irrevocable trusts, as the legal requirements can be complex.
2. Choose Trustees Wisely: Select trustees who can act impartially and in the best interests of the beneficiaries.
3. Consider Your Goals: Work closely with your attorney to define the specific goals you wish to achieve with the irrevocable trust, such as tax reduction, asset protection, or charitable giving.

Special Needs Trusts

1. Preserving Government Benefits: Special needs trusts are designed to provide for individuals with disabilities without jeopardizing their eligibility for government benefits such as Medicaid or Supplemental Security Income (SSI).

2. Supplemental Expenses: These trusts can cover additional expenses not provided by government programs, enhancing the quality of life for individuals with special needs.
3. Designated Trustees: Special needs trusts typically have trustees responsible for managing trust assets and making distributions on behalf of the beneficiary.

Suggestions:
1. Legal Expertise: Consult an attorney experienced in special needs planning to create a trust that complies with federal and state laws. The state specific requirements combined with potential Federal program requirements can create a maze of language needed to comply with both.
2. Clearly Define Beneficiary Needs: Work closely with the beneficiary and caregivers to outline the specific needs and preferences that the trust should address.
3. Consider Professional Trustees: Given the complex legal and financial requirements of special needs trusts, consider appointing a professional trustee or a trusted family member who has experience in this area.

Charitable Remainder Trusts

1. Supporting Charitable Causes: Charitable remainder trusts allow you to support a charity of your choice while retaining income from the trust during your lifetime or for a specified term.
2. Tax Benefits: Depending on how the trust is structured, you may receive an income tax deduction for the charitable contribution or reduce your estate tax liability.
3. Income Stream: These trusts can provide you with a reliable income stream during retirement or other periods of your life.

Suggestions:
1. Selecting Charities: Carefully research and choose the charitable organizations you wish to support, ensuring they align with your values and goals.
2. Financial Planning: Consult with financial and legal advisors to

determine the most tax-efficient way to structure the trust to benefit both you and the charity.
3. Documentation: Ensure that all legal and financial documentation related to the charitable remainder trust is correctly executed and filed.

Family Limited Partnerships (FLPs)

1. Asset Management and Control: FLPs are commonly used for family businesses and investment purposes to facilitate the controlled transfer of assets within a family while maintaining centralized control.
2. Tax Benefits: They can provide tax benefits, such as valuation discounts, which can reduce gift and estate tax liability.
3. Limited Partners and General Partners: FLPs typically have general partners who maintain control and limited partners who have a passive ownership role.

Suggestions:
1. Professional Guidance: Consult with an attorney and tax advisor to establish and manage the FLP, ensuring compliance with both legal and tax regulations.
2. Transparent Communication: Maintain open communication with family members involved in the partnership to avoid disputes and ensure everyone understands their roles and responsibilities.
3. Regular Reviews: Periodically review and update the FLP to reflect changes in family dynamics, financial goals, and estate planning objectives.

Chapter 4 – The Big Picture:

Incorporating trusts into your estate plan can be highly beneficial, but it's crucial to understand each trust's purpose and implications fully. Seek professional guidance when considering trust options, as the complexity of these instruments requires careful planning and execution to achieve your estate planning goals effectively. Regularly review and update your trust documents to ensure they align with your evolving financial and personal circumstances.

CHAPTER 5:
ESTATE AND GIFT TAX

Estate and gift taxes are critical considerations in estate planning, especially for individuals with significant assets. Understanding estate and gift taxes is crucial for effective estate planning and essential for effective wealth preservation and distribution. While most people won't be subject to these taxes, it's essential to be aware of the thresholds and rules. Below, we'll expand on estate tax, gift tax, and state-specific concerns, along with suggestions to address common tax-related concerns:

Estate Tax

1. Threshold and Exemption: As of 2023, the federal estate tax applied to estates exceeding $12.92 million per individual (or $25.84 million for married couples). This means that estates below these thresholds generally do not owe federal estate taxes.
2. Progressive Tax Rates: Estate tax rates are progressive, meaning that the tax rate increases as the estate's value exceeds certain tiers.
3. Portability: For married couples, the unused portion of the first spouse's exemption can be "ported" to the surviving spouse, effectively doubling the exemption amount for the surviving spouse.

ESTATE PLANNING BASICS: A BEGINNERS GUIDE

Suggestions:
1. Estate Planning Strategies: Consult with an estate planning attorney to explore strategies for minimizing estate tax liability. This may include the use of trusts (such as credit shelter trusts or qualified personal residence trusts), gifting strategies, and charitable giving.
2. Regular Review: Continuously monitor the value of your estate and the current estate tax thresholds, as these figures can change over time with new legislation. <u>The current exemption was doubled under the Tax Cuts and Jobs Act (TCJA) and is set to expire after 2025, unless statutorily amended.</u>
3. Beneficiary Designations: Review and update beneficiary designations on retirement accounts and life insurance policies to ensure they align with your estate planning goals.

<u>Gift Tax</u>

1. Annual Gift Tax Exclusion: The annual gift exclusion is a set amount that you may gift someone without having to report it to the IRS on a gift tax return. In 2023, you can give up to $17,000 to someone in a year without having to deal with the IRS.
2. Lifetime Gift Tax Exemption: In addition to the annual exclusion, there is a lifetime gift tax exemption, which was aligned with the estate tax exemption at $12.92 million per individual in 2023. This means you can gift up to this amount over your lifetime without paying gift tax.
3. Gift Splitting: Married couples can "split" gifts, allowing them to combine their annual exclusions and make larger tax-free gifts.

Suggestions:
1. Leverage Annual Exclusions: Consider gifting up to the annual exclusion amount to beneficiaries each year to reduce your taxable estate gradually.
2. Maximize Lifetime Exemption: For larger gifts, use your lifetime gift tax exemption. Keep in mind that this exemption may also be subject to changes in the law.
3. Document Gifts: Properly document all gifts to provide a clear record for both you and the IRS.

4. Consult with a Tax Professional: Complex gift transactions or those near the annual exclusion limit should be discussed with a tax professional to ensure compliance with tax laws.

State Estate and Inheritance Taxes

1. Varied State Laws: Some states impose their estate or inheritance taxes, and these laws vary widely. State exemption thresholds and tax rates can differ significantly from federal regulations.
2. No Federal Deduction: Unlike federal estate tax, state estate and inheritance taxes generally do not allow for a deduction from the federal estate tax paid.

Suggestions:
1. State-Specific Knowledge: Be aware of your state's estate tax laws, especially if you reside in a state with its own estate or inheritance tax.
2. Professional Guidance: Consult with a local estate planning attorney who is well-versed in your state's tax laws to ensure your estate plan aligns with state-specific requirements.
3. Regular Review: As state laws can change, periodically review your estate plan with an attorney to ensure it remains current and effective in minimizing state tax liabilities.

Estate and gift taxes are complex and subject to change due to legislative developments. Regularly reviewing your estate plan, staying informed about tax law changes, and consulting with experienced professionals are essential steps in managing estate and gift tax concerns. Additionally, consider using a combination of strategies, including trusts, gifting, and charitable planning, to optimize your estate plan while minimizing tax liabilities.

CHAPTER 6:
BENEFICIARY DESIGNATIONS

Beneficiary designations are a critical aspect of estate planning, as they determine who will receive specific assets upon your passing. It's crucial to handle these designations with care to avoid potential pitfalls and ensure your assets go to the intended recipients. Let's expand on these points and provide suggestions to address common concerns associated with beneficiary designations:

Keep Beneficiary Designations Current

1. Life Changes: Major life events, such as marriage, divorce, the birth of children, or the death of a beneficiary, can impact your beneficiary designations.
2. Primary and Contingent Beneficiaries: It's important to designate both primary and contingent (or secondary) beneficiaries. Contingent beneficiaries receive assets if the primary beneficiaries are unable to inherit.

Suggestions:
1. Regular Review: Periodically review your beneficiary designations, especially after significant life changes, to ensure they reflect your

current intentions.
2. Document Changes: Whenever you update beneficiary designations, keep records of the changes, including the date and any relevant documentation.
3. Beneficiary Relationships: Consider discussing your beneficiary designations with the individuals involved to avoid surprises and ensure everyone is aware of your intentions.

Avoid Common Mistakes

1. Naming Minors: Designating minors as direct beneficiaries can lead to complications, as they may not be able to manage inherited assets until they reach the age of majority.
2. Failure to Update: Failing to update beneficiary designations after significant life changes can result in assets going to unintended beneficiaries.
3. Failure to Understand Tax Implications: Certain assets, like retirement accounts, may have tax consequences for beneficiaries if not handled correctly.

Suggestions:
1. Create a Trust: If you want to leave assets to minors, consider establishing a trust and naming the trust as the beneficiary. This allows you to specify how the assets should be managed for the minor's benefit.
2. Stay Informed: Understand the tax implications of different beneficiary designations and consult with a tax professional or estate planning attorney to make informed decisions.
3. Periodic Checkups: Regularly review your beneficiary designations, ideally as part of a comprehensive annual review of your estate plan.

Coordinate with Your Estate Plan

1. Consistency: Ensure that your beneficiary designations align with the provisions of your will, trust, and other estate planning documents.
2. Avoid Conflicts: Conflicting beneficiary designations can lead to

disputes and potentially result in assets not being distributed as you intended.

Suggestions:
1. Consult with an Attorney: Work closely with an estate planning attorney to create and maintain beneficiary designations that are consistent with your overall estate plan.
2. Provide Copies: Share copies of your beneficiary designations with your attorney and the executor of your estate to ensure they are aware of your wishes and can facilitate a smooth asset transfer.
3. Communication: Clearly communicate your beneficiary designations and estate plan to your family members and loved ones to minimize the potential for disputes or misunderstandings.

Chapter 6 – The Big Picture:

Beneficiary designations are a crucial component of estate planning. Regularly reviewing and updating these designations, avoiding common mistakes, and ensuring consistency with your overall estate plan are vital steps in managing your assets and ensuring they pass to your chosen beneficiaries according to your wishes. Seek professional guidance when needed, and maintain open communication with family members and loved ones to ensure everyone is on the same page regarding your beneficiary designations and estate plan.

CHAPTER 7:
ADVANCED HEALTHCARE DIRECTIVES AND POWERS OF ATTORNEY

Advanced healthcare directives and powers of attorney are critical components of estate planning that address your medical preferences and decision-making authority in times of incapacity. These documents ensure your wishes are respected and that trusted individuals can act on your behalf. Let's delve into each document and provide suggestions to avoid common pitfalls when incorporating them into a comprehensive estate plan:

<u>Living Will</u>

1. Terminal Illness or Unconsciousness: A living will specifies your preferences regarding life-sustaining treatments when facing a terminal illness or permanent unconsciousness.
2. Treatment Choices: It allows you to express whether you want treatments such as mechanical ventilation, artificial nutrition, or cardiopulmonary resuscitation (CPR) to be administered or withheld under specific circumstances.

Suggestions:
1. Clarity: Be explicit in your living will, clearly outlining your

preferences for various medical interventions.
2. Consult with Healthcare Professionals: Discuss your choices with your healthcare providers to ensure you fully understand the implications of your decisions.
3. Review and Update: Periodically review and update your living will to reflect any changes in your medical preferences or state laws.

Healthcare Power of Attorney

1. Designated Decision-Maker: A healthcare power of attorney allows you to appoint someone as your healthcare agent or proxy who can make medical decisions on your behalf when you are unable to do so.
2. Broad Decision-Making Authority: Your agent has the authority to make healthcare decisions, including choices not explicitly covered in your living will.

Suggestions:
1. Trust and Communication: Select a healthcare agent you trust implicitly and with whom you have discussed your medical preferences. Open communication is key.
2. Provide Copies: Give copies of your healthcare power of attorney to your healthcare providers to ensure they recognize your agent's authority.
3. Consider Alternates: Appoint alternate agents in case your primary agent is unavailable or unwilling to serve.

HIPAA Authorization

1. Privacy Protection: The Health Insurance Portability and Accountability Act (HIPAA) Authorization allows healthcare providers to disclose your medical information to individuals you designate.
2. Access to Information: Without this authorization, your agents may encounter obstacles when trying to access your medical records or communicate with healthcare providers.

Suggestions:
1. Execute HIPAA Authorization: Ensure you complete a HIPAA authorization form as part of your estate plan.
2. Provide Copies: Share copies of the HIPAA authorization with your designated healthcare agents and keep one in your medical records.
3. Inform Agents: Make sure your agents are aware of the existence of this authorization and its significance in facilitating their role.

General Durable Power of Attorney

1. Financial Affairs: A general durable power of attorney appoints someone to manage your financial affairs and make decisions on your behalf if you become incapacitated.
2. Comprehensive Authority: This document can grant broad authority or be limited to specific financial matters, depending on your preferences.

Suggestions:
1. Choose a Trustworthy Agent: Appoint an agent you trust to act in your best financial interests. Financial powers of attorney can be highly sensitive.
2. Clarity and Limitations: Clearly define the scope of your agent's authority and any limitations to avoid potential misuse.
3. Consider Professional Guidance: Consult with an attorney or financial advisor to ensure your financial power of attorney is structured correctly and complies with state laws.

Incorporating these advanced healthcare directives and powers of attorney into your estate plan is vital for ensuring your medical and financial preferences are honored in times of incapacity. Regularly review and update these documents, and ensure that your designated agents are aware of their responsibilities and have access to the necessary documentation. Additionally, consult with an experienced estate planning attorney to create these documents effectively and in accordance with your specific needs and state laws.

CHAPTER 8:
REVIEW AND UPDATE YOUR ESTATE PLAN

Estate planning is dynamic, and it's crucial to regularly review and update your plan to ensure it continues to align with your goals, circumstances, and the evolving legal landscape. Here, we'll provide additional details for each subsection and offer suggestions to avoid common pitfalls when incorporating these considerations into a comprehensive estate plan:

<u>Major Life Events Occur</u>

1. Births: The birth of a child or grandchild may require updates to include new beneficiaries, guardianship designations, or changes to trusts.
2. Deaths: The passing of a spouse, family member, or designated beneficiary necessitates revisions to your plan, such as designating new heirs or adjusting bequests.
3. Marriages: Entering a marriage may involve updating beneficiary designations, considering spousal rights, and potentially creating or amending prenuptial agreements.
4. Divorces: A divorce typically requires significant revisions, including changes to beneficiaries, distribution of assets, and updates to powers of attorney.

5. Financial Changes: Significant changes in your financial situation, such as the acquisition of new assets, sale of property, or changes in investments, may necessitate adjustments to your estate plan.

Suggestions:
1. Frequent Review: Conduct regular reviews of your estate plan, ideally on an annual basis, to ensure it remains current.
2. Consult with Professionals: Seek guidance from an estate planning attorney when major life events occur, as they can help you make the necessary updates while ensuring compliance with legal requirements.
3. Maintain Documentation: Keep records of all changes and updates to your estate plan, including the dates and reasons for each modification.

Tax Laws Change

1. Federal and State Tax Laws: Tax laws are subject to change at both the federal and state levels, impacting estate tax thresholds, exemptions, and planning strategies.
2. Income Tax Implications: Changes in tax laws may also affect income tax considerations for your estate, such as capital gains tax on the sale of assets.

Suggestions:
1. Stay Informed: Regularly monitor tax law changes and consider subscribing to updates from reputable sources or consulting with tax professionals.
2. Proactive Planning: When tax laws change, consult with your estate planning attorney to proactively adjust your plan to optimize tax benefits and minimize liabilities.

Beneficiary Relationships Change

1. Beneficiary Needs: Over time, your beneficiaries' financial needs and circumstances may change, requiring adjustments to inheritance plans.

2. Changing Dynamics: Relationships among beneficiaries can evolve, potentially necessitating changes in distribution or trusts.
3. Beneficiary Health: Changes in the health or well-being of beneficiaries may prompt updates to your healthcare directives and guardianship provisions.

Suggestions:
1. Open Communication: Maintain open communication with your beneficiaries to understand their evolving needs and financial situations.
2. Periodic Conversations: Schedule periodic discussions with your estate planning attorney to assess whether changes are necessary to align your plan with beneficiary dynamics.
3. Flexibility: Consider incorporating flexibility into your estate plan, allowing your executor or trustee to make discretionary decisions based on the beneficiaries' changing circumstances.

Regularly reviewing and updating your estate plan is a vital part of responsible estate planning. Neglecting to adapt your plan to major life events, changing tax laws, and beneficiary relationships can result in unintended consequences and legal challenges. Seek professional guidance, stay informed, and maintain a proactive approach to ensure your estate plan remains effective in achieving your goals and protecting your loved ones.

CHAPTER 9: CONCLUSION

Estate planning is a comprehensive and ongoing process that requires thoughtful consideration, meticulous documentation, and regular review. By understanding the fundamental concepts discussed in this book, you have taken significant steps toward safeguarding your legacy and ensuring your wishes are respected in the future. From defining the scope of your assets and minimizing tax burdens to creating wills, trusts, and advanced directives, you now possess the knowledge to navigate the intricate terrain of estate planning.

Remember that estate planning is not a one-size-fits-all endeavor; it's a dynamic and highly personalized journey. Life is filled with changes—some joyful, others challenging—and your estate plan should evolve alongside them. Embrace major life events as opportunities to revisit and refine your plan, ensuring it reflects your current priorities and the needs of your loved ones. Stay vigilant regarding changes in tax laws and beneficiary relationships, and always seek professional guidance when necessary.

By investing the time and effort to craft a well-considered estate plan, you provide your family with the gift of clarity during difficult times and leave a lasting legacy that reflects your values and aspirations. Your legacy is not only the wealth you pass down but also the wisdom, love, and care that you impart to those you hold dear. Through responsible estate planning, you have taken a meaningful step toward preserving and protecting both your financial assets and the well-being of your family for generations to come.

As you embark on your estate planning journey, remember that the knowledge and insights within these chapters serve as a foundation for informed decision-making. Seek professional guidance from estate planning attorneys, tax advisors, and financial planners who can provide personalized strategies tailored to your unique circumstances. With the right support and a well-structured estate plan, you can enjoy the peace of mind that comes from knowing your legacy is in capable hands.

PLANNING OUTLINE

An intake questionnaire for estate planning is a valuable tool to gather essential information from clients to help an attorney or estate planner create a customized estate plan. This questionnaire should cover various aspects of a person's financial and personal life. Please use the outline below to help you in organizing all the necessary information to better prepare for the planning process:

Client Information:

- Client's Full Name:
- Client's Date of Birth:
- Client's Social Security Number:
- Client's Address:
- Client's Phone Number:
- Client's Email Address:

Spouse/Partner Information (if applicable):

- Spouse/Partner's Full Name:
- Spouse/Partner's Date of Birth:
- Spouse/Partner's Social Security Number:

- Spouse/Partner's Address (if different from the client's):
- Spouse/Partner's Phone Number:
- Spouse/Partner's Email Address:

Children and Dependents:

- Child/Dependent Name:
- Relationship to Client:
- Date of Birth:
- Social Security Number:

(Repeat this section for each child or dependent.)

Healthcare Planning:

Do you have any specific healthcare directives in place (e.g., living will, healthcare power of attorney)?
- If yes, please provide copies.

Financial Information:

- Income Sources:
    - Please list all sources of income, including employment, investments, pensions, and rental income.

- Bank Accounts:
    - List all bank accounts, including account numbers and current balances.

- Investments:
    - Provide details of your investments, including stocks, bonds, mutual funds, and retirement accounts (e.g., 401(k), IRA).

- Real Estate:
    - List all real estate properties you own, including primary

residence, vacation homes, and investment properties. Include property values and outstanding mortgages.

- Business Interests:
  - If you own a business, provide details, including the type of business, ownership percentage, and estimated value.

- Other Assets:
  - Mention any other significant assets, such as vehicles, valuable collectibles, or intellectual property.

- Debts and Liabilities:
  - List all debts and liabilities, including mortgages, loans, credit card debt, and any other financial obligations.

Estate Planning Goals:

What are your primary goals for your estate plan?
- (e.g., asset distribution, minimizing taxes, healthcare directives, guardianship for minor children, charitable giving)

Executor and Trustees:

Who would you like to appoint as the executor of your will?
- (Name and contact information)

If applicable, who would you like to appoint as trustees for any trusts you plan to establish?
- (Name and contact information for each trustee)

Guardianship (if applicable):

Who would you like to designate as the guardian(s) for your minor children in case of your incapacity or passing?
- (Name and contact information)

Charitable Giving:

Do you have any specific charitable organizations you'd like to include in your estate plan?
- (Name of organization, purpose, and contact information)

Additional Comments:

Is there any other information or specific concerns you'd like to discuss regarding your estate planning?

By using this intake questionnaire, estate planning professionals can gather the necessary information to create a comprehensive and tailored estate plan that aligns with the client's goals and circumstances. It also ensures that the client's wishes are clearly understood and can be legally documented.

ABOUT THE AUTHOR

David Russ is a practicing attorney with Pierce Law Group, PLLC. He graduated from the Norman Adrian Wiggins School of Law at Campbell University. He is married to his law school sweetheart and lives in Durham with his wife and three children. His practice includes all of the state of North Carolina and focuses primarily on developing estate and inheritance plans for a wide variety of clients.

Made in the USA
Columbia, SC
20 December 2023